Every Student Has a Story

Personal Narratives from
First-Generation College Students

TRIO Student Support Services

Edited and Coordinated by
Karen Lenfestey and Shubitha Kever

Cover Design by
Emily Salisbury

ISBN-10: 1537570323
ISBN-13: 978-1537570327

DEDICATION

When you're the first person in your family to do something, many obstacles can stand in your way. This book is dedicated to all of the first-generation college students who struggle to fit-in, who sometimes wonder if they should quit, but who persevere and work diligently to succeed and overcome.

INTRODUCTION

This book is a compilation of essays by TRIO Student Support Services Students at Indiana University Purdue University Fort Wayne (IPFW). Inspired by Aquinas College's student publishing project, IPFW TRIO Student Support Services coordinated a semester long opportunity for TRIO students in the spring of 2016. Students were asked to participate in writing circles where they could tell their stories, hear other students' stories, and get feedback about how to write compelling essays about their life experiences. Students were simply asked:

What has it been like for you being the first person in your family to go to college?

What struggles have you faced and what have you learned from those struggles?

The stories and subsequent essays these questions generated far exceeded the project's expectations. These essays are now combined in this powerful collection in the hope that they will resonate with other first-generation students who often feel as though they don't fit in and who struggle but keep pressing forward.

Along with allowing students to tell their stories, this process has helped students develop meaningful friendships with their peers and gain a greater sense of self-confidence in their writing abilities. But even more importantly, this process has cultivated a greater sense of pride for students related to their personal experiences and their many successes and triumphs.

EVERY STUDENT HAS A STORY

CONTENTS

THE OUTCAST
BY KRISTIN COSTELLO

A.S.H.'s parents: "Hey! Let's go out to eat."
The girls: "Yeah, where should we go?"
A.S.H.'s parents: "How about Mexican?"
The girls: "Sure!"

I don't have money to go out to eat! I know they invited me, but I've been saving for almost a year and barely have enough money to stock up on groceries! Going out to eat was always considered a luxury in my family.

These were the first thoughts I had the first day I moved into my college dorm.

My roommate's parents drove us to the restaurant and every entrée the girls and my roommate's parents ordered was over $10. They acted like it was normal to go out and spend that much money on their meals. Growing up, my family never went out to eat. My brother and I were always taught to cook our own food; and, I would often just eat the free food at the restaurant where I worked (nearly full-time) throughout high school. I was never certain if there was going to be food in the fridge at home.

At the end of our meal my new roommate's parents paid the bill. *How could they afford to pay for that entire bill and why would they pay that entire bill?*

After being accepted to college and making the arrangements to move my entire life to Fort Wayne, Indiana, I got to room with three middle-class, white females. These females had never been exposed to such diversity in their lives and now they lived with someone so different from them. Different in the color of their skin, different in the amount of money they came from, and different in where they came from. I felt like I was defined as a broke, first-generation, Mexican girl from the Chicagoland area.

My grandma, grandpa, and mom drove me to Fort Wayne. My fresh start. They came upstairs to meet my new roommates' parents and I could immediately feel the awkwardness and tension. The way we talked, the way we looked, everything about us was different from them.

My mother has always been a very outspoken woman and for some reason that day she barely spoke at all. My grandma and grandpa just didn't really know how to make conversation with those kind of people: the richie, white-looking kind of people. After moving all my totes in, my family decided they were heading back to Chicago. I walked them downstairs, gave them hugs and kissed them goodbye. We waved and told each other we'd keep in touch and that was it.

In my three years attending IPFW, I've struggled with being an outcast on more than one occasion. After getting more comfortable with my roommates, they began to make subtle comments on the way I talked or said things. They would refer to me as "ghetto." It was funny to them, but to me it was not. I don't think they truly knew what that term meant. The way I talked was how the people back home did; it's just how I grew up. They would comment on the way I said things like when I would say "init" instead of "isn't it" or "o'girl/o'boy" instead of the male or female's name I was actually referring to. When the topic of my race would come up they would always ask why I never spoke Spanish. Not only my roommates, but many other students I met my first year of college. They would say "but you're Mexican, aren't you supposed to speak Spanish?" or even more often than not, they would tell me I didn't even look Mexican, I looked "Asian."

My roommates would share with me how there were only two or three black people that went to their high school. The neighborhoods I had always lived in were mostly minorities; and I was used to being submerged in diverse cultures growing up. They didn't go to diverse schools or live in communities with many minorities. One girl's parents would make comments towards Mexicans and blacks; and my roommates would share with me the comments they had made. It was as if they thought the comments their parents made were funny; but to me, it was just racist.

So, not only did I feel as an outcast because of the color of my skin, the way that I talked and the neighborhoods I had lived in, but what more could possibly make me feel the way I did? The topic of money.

Sometimes, the girls would ask me to go out to eat with them or go to the mall; but when I would tell them I didn't have money to go do stuff like that, they would ask me why I couldn't just ask my family for some money. This is when I began to realize more and more how different I was from these girls and how much more I felt like an outcast.

I had finally begun to accept the fact that I was roomed with three middle-class, white females who never worried about money, who never had an issue with their race or the way they talked, and who never knew what it was like to live amongst minorities. Their parents paid for their tuition, their living expenses, and/or their necessities, while I couldn't even ask my mom to send me $5.

All three of my roommates were fortunate to have both of their parents in their lives, some of which had gone to college. I was first-generation in my family and my parents got a divorce when I was in second grade. My dad gained custody of my brother and I, but had passed when I was just 15. This was just one more thing I felt divided us. They had no understanding of what it was like to have separated parents nor to lose one of them at an early age. See? Differences.

Although I felt like an outcast my freshman year of college, I learned to not focus on the differences between me and my college roommates in a negative way, but in a positive way. You may ask how that is even possible. Well, I learned to watch the way I talked and made the changes necessary as to not be called "ghetto" as often as I did that first year. I got a job on campus my second semester so as not to worry so much about my financial situation and focus more on my studies. I may not be able to change the color of my skin or where I came from, but I used my past to progress my future. Being and feeling like an outcast gave me the motivation to change myself. Not for the girls I was roomed with, but for myself. I no longer wanted to be seen as an outcast. I wanted to be seen as an inspirer and an achiever.

I began to get more involved on campus and find ways to submerge myself in more diversity. I joined groups and programs and even became a mentor. I now work full-time and continue to earn a higher GPA than I ever did in high school. If anyone could relate to my story in any way, I just want you to know that you can do it. I am not an outcast. I am just a little unique and I am my own person. I came to college to better my life and create a fresh start. I came here to break tradition and to succeed as a first-generation student. So for those of you who have ever felt as an outcast, I am here to tell you it's okay. I was there. But now, I am here. I'm doing it. I'm breaking tradition. I am first-generation.

SURVIVAL OF THE FITTEST
BY LORENZO CATALAN

Where I am from, some people don't make it. When I was younger, people would tell me that I'd be dead or in jail in a few years. I never thought my neighborhood was a bad place, until I realized that crime like that didn't happen everywhere. When I saw the effects of the environment (hanging out with people in gangs, committing crimes, selling drugs and using drugs) take a toll on my brother, I just knew I needed to escape. I needed better.

While I was in 7th grade, an event changed my life. I was watching a Tyler Perry movie, one where one of the kids was dealing drugs, something went wrong, and he was shot in an alley. During that part of the movie, it hit me, almost as if the bullet had come through the TV and ripped through my skin. I thought to myself "Why is this so emotional for me? It's just a movie, like yeah, Tyler Perry makes good movies but dang, it's not even that deep."

About 10 minutes later there was a knock at the door and there was a kid, about my age who said, "Aren't you _____'s brother?"

I replied, "Yeah. Why?"

"Your brother was just shot and he's in an ambulance on his way to the hospital right now."

I felt as if I had an out of body experience and I was looking down on myself wondering what was happening. My brother and I were close, as both of our fathers had abandoned their posts. He was my role model. I had just seen him that day; could he really be gone?

Later, my mom and I went to the hospital to visit him; but he wasn't the brother I knew. That brother was invincible and no one could hurt him. This kid here couldn't even breathe on his own and looked like he only had a few more breaths left in him. If the monitor was not letting me know his heart was beating, I would have thought he was dead. From that very moment, looking at him in the hospital bed, with only inches of life left, I knew I needed an escape, I needed better. That's when I decided to go to college.

[Fast forward 5 years]

My very first week on campus was amazing. There were events to get to know other students, and since I'm a social creature, I was thriving. I was absolutely loving it here. Every day there was something new to do. Yes, I went to class but I didn't come back to my dorm and do my homework like I should've. It felt just like high school with more fun and more freedom. I hung out with my friends every day and avoided my obligations.

18

Growing up as a low income student, there were a lot of things that I went without and being in college, there were opportunities to have those things. For example, as stupid as this is, it really did set me back. At the library you could check out a laptop or IPad. I checked out an IPad because I just wanted to see how it worked. It may have been the very first day of school that I checked an IPad out, downloaded the social media apps and I was on it for 6 hours. Yes, it does sound ridiculous but I was. It continued like that for about 3-5 weeks. That's how I spent my free time during the week. On the weekends, I would hang out with my girlfriend because I no longer got to see her every day now that I was away in college.

Once I wanted to give up the IPad, it became like an addiction and I couldn't just stop. I had 5 weeks of reading to do, a test in a few days and I was unprepared. Of course, I failed the test. I began to have anxiety and doubt whether I was even supposed to be in college. No one in my immediate or extended family had ever gone to college. I felt as if I was kidding myself being here. I felt as if I was just a joke and everyone could see right through me. I had heard how difficult pre-med was but I had been naive. Suddenly, I thought about giving up my dream of becoming a doctor. Considering I had procrastinated throughout basically half of the semester at this point I was just playing catch up. I went to class and I could not comprehend what was happening. I felt so lost and stupid and like I didn't belong here. I was overwhelmed by the amount of work. I missed my family, and I would cry and have an emotional breakdown every Monday and Tuesday because those were the days that the obligations of school really hit me. There used to be a show on ABC called Wipe Out where contestants would go through an obstacle course and the thing I found most comical was when a person was running head on and a big bouncy ball was thrown in their face and they flipped backwards. That is what college felt like for me. I had amazing intentions and I was running through; but then, it all hit me. Part of me just wanted to drop out. Part of me just wanted a way to make things easier.

My worries only got worse from there because I was about half way through the semester, failing about every quiz and test in my chemistry class. The class was a 4 credit hour class; and if I didn't get those credits, I would have dropped from 14 credit hours to 10. Then, I would have become a part time student and lose the financial aid I got as a full time student. This added to my worries because I had no other way to pay for college. I would have had to drop out at that point.

Throughout all of these struggles, I was having weekly appointments with my TRIO advisor and she was helping me through it. Before I wasn't listening as I should've been, but now I had to. She then suggested I stop getting an IPad. As I said, as dumb as it may seem, this technology was going to keep me from passing my class and from graduating on time, so I just stopped cold turkey. She also suggested making a checklist. I previously shared with her that I was aware of the assignments I needed to do, but they were all in my head. Just thinking about them, made everything overwhelming and that stressed me out and was the cause of the breakdowns. The day I stopped checking out the IPad, I took her advice. In my head there were at least 20 things to do but on paper there were only 5. I labeled them with A (as needed done today) and B (would be good to get done today but can wait for tomorrow). I did that and got things done. It was week 8 when I made that change. Things started to look up from there. I began to believe in myself because I found these videos on YouTube by Les Brown, Wayne Dyer, Ray Lewis, Eric Thomas and others. They motivated me and were exactly what I needed. I was still failing my chem quizzes, but I was failing with a higher score than before. I was improving and it made me happier. I had stopped hanging out with my girlfriend as much. I stopped using the IPad and I started using a checklist. I managed to end that class with a C- (which was the minimum requirement for my biology degree). I continued my new habits into the new semester. Now, I use my syllabi as a checklist and actually do the readings. When I stopped procrastinating, I stopped feeling overwhelmed and stressed. Everything is much better.

Looking back through the years, I could have never imagined that I, a Hispanic male from a bad neighborhood, who was expected to be dead or in jail, would be here in college pursuing my dream. College provides the opportunity for me to be someone different, someone better and I just have to take advantage of it. Focusing on my priorities is how I will do it and my why is so I can make the world a better place. As a biology major, a quote by Charles Darwin really resonates with me: "It is not the strongest of the species that survives, nor the most intelligent, but the one most responsive to change." Everything is hard in the beginning. It's something we have never done before and no one we know has ever done it before; so we don't know what to expect. No matter how bad it is or how bad it gets, you're going to make it. You just have to reassess your priorities, learn to say no to those things or people that waste your time, and find out your why for being here.

THEY SAY
BY BRITTEN FRIAR

Trailer trash. That's what my classmates called me in elementary school. "My mom says I can't play with you," they'd say. "Your family is poor and trashy." I felt like an outcast, and I believed them.

"She's such a good writer," my fourth grade teacher told my parents. "Where did she learn to write like that? She has a real talent," she'd say. I felt special, and I believed her.

"College, she's got to go to college," I overheard my parents saying when I was 13. I thought that was pretty unfair; neither of them had gone to college and they seemed fine. "No kid of mine is going to work a job where their name is sewn on their shirt," my dad would say. I didn't know what that meant, but he sounded serious so I believed him.

"At risk" is how my counselor described me my senior year of high school. In notes and phone calls home she'd say, "Britten is at serious risk to lose her Honor's Diploma. She was doing great until this year . . . if she doesn't get her act together, she may not graduate at all." I felt like a failure, and I believed her.

Accepted. That's what they wrote at the top of my letter from IPFW. All of my relatives called to tell me how proud they were, excited that I would be the first in my family to go to college. I was scared, but I believed them.

My life, not unlike your life, has had its ups and downs. I have grown so much over the years. I have made major mistakes, and I have lost people close to me. I have set goals for myself and stuck to them. I've gotten more involved in school, gained valuable life experiences, and made life-long friends. I have often doubted myself and my ability to succeed. I've done things I never thought possible for a trailer trash kid like me (like traveling to Puerto Rico to volunteer and applying for the Peace Corps). All of these things make me who I am today.

I'll never forget where I came from, or all of the people who have helped me on my journey. I don't know what they are all saying about me now, but I do know this: I say that I am capable of anything I set my mind to, despite the challenges or obstacles I may face.

And I believe me.

EMBRACING EVERY PART OF YOU

BY EMILY SALISBURY

At my regular Thursday night art class, a few semesters ago, something quite bizarre occurred. I was sitting at my table, just sketching away when I felt my chest tighten. My heart started beating intensely out of control. I glanced around the room quickly, checking to see if anyone else noticed before I got up and ran to the bathroom. When I got there, I ran past another girl, locked myself in a stall and grabbed at my raging heart. My breathing rate escalated and I began to hyperventilate. I felt like my heart was going to explode.

After I knew I was finally alone, I left the stall and went over to the sink. I splashed some cold water on my face and wrists and checked my pulse. My heart was beating at an alarming 111 bpm. I gripped the sink and stared back at my pale face, while my chest wheezed for air. I was having a full blown panic attack. More specifically, I was having my first un-triggered panic attack.

Hi, I'm Emily and I have GAD, or better known as Generalized Anxiety Disorder. I have only been clinically diagnosed with my anxiety disorder for about a year and a half now, but I have been living with a milder sense of anxiety my whole life. I have also been known to have panic attacks in the past, but they have always been "triggered," which basically just means that my panic is caused by a specific situation. My fall semester of 2015 was the first time in my entire life that I had ever had an un-triggered panic attack and it terrified me. That entire semester I had been struggling with my anxiety and about a week before my incident, I had a sharp pain building in my chest that ultimately lead to my panic attack. The fact that it was a surprise absolutely terrified me.

Following my incident, I eventually opened up to my Thursday night professor and told him about my intense anxiety. I believe that is the moment when my mindset about my mental disorder changed. One of his common quotes was along the lines of "embrace the stress of this environment; you'll never get another chance to live through this kind of environment again." Those words were very inspiring to me and really made me think about my anxiety and ultimately reevaluate how I thought about it.

For my final project in one of my art classes during that semester, I ended up deciding to center my project on my anxiety. I figured it was about time for me to begin embracing my anxiety and learning how to channel it into something good, rather than see it as a crippling issue. During my final critique I was definitely scared, but I also felt incredibly empowered. I could not hide which piece of art work was mine and you know what? I was okay with that.

Nowadays, I still don't understand my anxiety fully, but I am gaining a better understanding of who I am with each difficult task I accomplish. Before I began embracing my anxiety, I typically stayed away from things that made me uncomfortable, for obvious reasons. However, with my new attitude I pushed myself out of my comfort zone and really got involved with a group on campus called TRIO. I am so thankful that I did, because I am finally in a place where other people can accept me for who I am. As a part of TRIO, I was even given the incredible opportunity to travel to the beautiful island of Puerto Rico. Even though I felt overwhelmed at times, I was still able to experience Puerto Rican culture through a variety of different ways, ranging from hiking through rainforests to meeting fellow TRIO students just like me. I have been opened up to so many new and exciting opportunities because I pushed myself to overcome my mental disorder; and the TRIO people that I have met have been so accepting of who I am. So, I guess what I am trying to say is, you are who you are and that includes every part of you. It may take time, but learn to embrace who you are and I promise you things will get better.

ONLY <u>YOU</u> CAN PREDICT YOUR FUTURE

BY BREANNA RENÉ PUTT

Growing up with a parent as a drug addict makes life harder than it should be. Being left at home alone to take care of my younger sister was expected. I formed more of a motherly role with her than an actual sister role which I'll carry on for the rest of my years. I can't really take back any of the sights or the things I heard growing up. I don't believe anyone should have to have gone through what I did: from being left alone while my mom was out; to growing up and getting a car and having to take my mom to her friends' so they could "hang out;" to trying to calm my sister down in the backseat when mom says to stay down or we'll get shot because we're in the ghetto part of the neighborhood so she could go inside the bar and buy drugs; to trying to answer questions about what my sister found in mom's purse.

Once my dad had gotten custody of my sister and me, things calmed down a bit. I was more able to concentrate on school and sports and not have to play that motherly role as much. However, for my mom, things expedited due to her not having any sense of 'responsibility' to deal with anymore. In a sense she sort of jumped off the deep end and we would barely hear from her when she was on her drug sprees. The most we heard from her was when she needed something or an excuse to get a ride somewhere. I still tried to protect my sister at this time from seeing the emotional abuse that was thrown at us. Talking to our mom while she was in jail, prison, or house arrest became normal for us. This was the only time we could actually talk to her without her wanting something else or there being an ulterior motive to visiting her. When she wasn't in trouble with the law we would barely get to talk to her and she only contacted us when she wanted something. My dad didn't like us seeing our mom, which was understandable; but he did not stop us because that was our mom. I am glad that he did not keep us from her and took the higher road in a sense. I do believe that if he didn't allow us to see her that we would've grown up to resent him for it.

Going through high school, I knew for a fact that I wanted to go to college and better myself. To be someone everyone thought I couldn't be. People assumed that because my mother was a drug addict that I should have been one too and followed in her footsteps. I went to college right after high school with the mind set of becoming a doctor. I realized fast that being a doctor wasn't for me, but what everyone else wanted for me. I didn't want to go to school that long; as well as, I hated the science courses that were required. I ended up changing my major three more times before I finally was happy with the degree I was going for.

While in college, I lived at my grandfather's house even though other relatives were not too fond of this idea. There was a lot of jealousy surrounding it due to me being the oldest grandchild and I wasn't supposed to turn out the way I did. Rumor was that I was going to 'take advantage' of my grandpa when in reality, it is a place to stay at while going to college. My grandfather, on the other hand, was excited for me to move in, that way he had company and wasn't necessarily all on his own. In a sense, we both kind of take care of each other.

Because of my past experiences and the cards I was dealt when I was younger, I knew I wanted to make a difference in someone's life. One program I was really interested in was Big Brothers Big Sisters. It is a program that mainly helps those children in poverty in need of someone to look up to, as well as to have someone outside of the family be there for them. I decided to finally get involved and I have been recently volunteering with this organization to help get myself out in the community and to give back. I know growing up, I went through a lot of things that kids shouldn't have to go through and I want to help someone else in case they may be going through their own challenges and need someone in their life they can always go to. I think it would be amazing to be that someone's go-to person to help make a difference in their life and that way they know they are not alone in this fight called life.

Now, I am currently a senior at Indiana University-Purdue University Fort Wayne (IPFW). I will be graduating this December (2016) with a bachelor's in public policy. I will be double majoring in health services administration and criminal justice as well as minoring in public affairs. I am blessed to work two full-time jobs in the healthcare field, in addition to my volunteering as a Big Sister. Even with working as much as I do, I still manage to make sure I pass my classes and so far that hasn't become an issue. The only regret I have going through college and working so much, is that I wish I would've gotten involved on campus more and participated in more school events.

As of today, my mother is a year and a half sober; and I am proud of her for that, as I know she is proud of me. I am thankful to have had my dad there for me throughout the years to be there for me and to give me hard criticism and that push when I needed it. If it wasn't for him, I don't believe that I would be as strong and bull headed as I am now. I am also grateful to have my grandpa there for me and always help me when I need it. He supports and brags about all that I have accomplished and continues to be proud of me, which is more than I can ask for. Being there for my sister and her being there for me in the best way we know how, has also helped me to become who I am. If I wasn't needed by her, I don't believe I'd be as responsible or caring as I am today. I am very proud of the person she has become as well, even if we do have our differences and can't agree on many things. I can also say that I am very thankful for what life has put me through because I would not be the strong person I am today if I had gone through life any other way. I strongly believe that we choose our own paths and it shouldn't matter what past we may have, what matters are the dreams we are shooting for.

TRIALS AND TRIBULATIONS
BY JO'MALE COLLIER

Life is full of trouble and everyone will have their piece. This is something that is unavoidable; however no matter how bad it may seem, giving up is never the answer. I was raised in South Bend, Indiana, where I lived with one of the most influential people in my life, my father. Growing up it was always my dream to become a doctor. I had spent all of my childhood around doctors because I was born with Osteogenesis Impefecta, which is a brittle bone disease. My disease had made me curious: I wanted to understand how it worked and why it worked.

In order to be a doctor, you have to get good grades; however, that wasn't a major concern of mine in elementary school until I saw my best friend rewarded for his. All I could think of is how I wanted a medal like his. Then once my grades improved, I received praise from my mom and my dad. I felt smart. I would bring home certificates with my name on them saying your son, Jo'Male Collier, has made high honor roll. My dad would always brag to his friends about me. My sister and I were my parents' greatest achievements, and they made sure that all of their friends and whoever else was around, knew it. No longer was I just trying to get a medal, but now I was trying to see how many awards I could get. I was never the smartest in my class, but I always aimed for it. I wanted to be the kid who sat down and knew every answer.

The roughest part of my childhood was my parents' arguments. If anything was happening in our neighborhood as far as arguments go, it was at my house. When my mom would get mad, an argument could last until the next morning. Things would get more stressful when my mom left; she had custody of my little sister so when she left, my sister went with her. Eventually they would come back and the cycle would repeat. There were those good times, too, when both of my parents got along: breakfast would be cooked, I would get help with my homework, and we ate together. It was a touch of what could have been. Somehow that made it worse because I could do nothing but wonder what happened. The bond between me and my parents, though complex, was very real. Through it all, I loved both of them and I would never choose to have different parents. Although my father and I butted heads from time to time because we were so much alike, he was always someone I looked up to and wanted to be like.

The biggest and worst devastation of my life came on June 30, 2011. It was a Thursday. Many times my father had been hospitalized for seizures and once for a bad reaction with his medication. Like all the other times, I thought he would come home and we would go back to hanging out, barbequing, having parties on the weekend, and playing with the other kids on the block, just like normal. This is not what happened at all. My sister and I had been taken to Fort Wayne, Indiana to stay with my aunt for a couple of days while my dad was in the hospital. When we returned to South Bend, we were told that our dad had not been doing so well. Sometime that morning, they'd pulled the plug on my father and he'd flat lined. It was terrible. All I wanted in that moment was for it to be a lie. I couldn't believe it. The person who I thought would never die had died. Your parents always tell you that they're not going to be here forever, that one day they'll pass away, but nothing can prepare you for it. Words don't come anywhere close to the actual event. So there we were. . . I was 15 and my sister, 11, now fatherless. Everything that I had known up until that moment came into question. It was like being hit by a semi-truck.

In addition to the stress of losing my father, I was making the challenging transition from middle school to high school. It was during this time that I fell into one of the worst depressions ever. I wanted my old life back. I didn't want to be anywhere but home looking at my dad sitting in his chair, in his spot in the kitchen at the table with the TV on. This however couldn't be. I wanted to go to sleep and for it to all be a bad dream. There are no words to describe this pain. Just writing about it is painful in itself. This isn't something that goes away like food poisoning or a bad rash. This is something you just learn to live with. My dad had passed and so did my drive to learn. It had always been my dream to find some way to extend the life of my dad so I would be able to have him for just a little while longer. He was dead now, so why try? Why do anything, but lay there in bed? In many ways I wanted to close my eyes at night, and not open them the next morning. Life wasn't worth it; my life wasn't worth it.

It was because of my family and Upward Bound that I made it through this tough time in my life. I avoided Upward Bound originally because I just wanted to relax and have fun. School was stress, and alcohol and stress had killed my father. It was hard making friends in high school, yet with Upward Bound, it was almost guaranteed. The Summer Program is what really got me because I was on my own and living with my peers. Nights of laughter and days of school. In the end, I ran to Upward Bound not for the education, but for the people. I didn't get back my drive for school right away, but I knew if I wanted to stay in Upward Bound, I had to have good grades.

Often times, I find myself stressed out now that I'm in my first year of college. Fortunately, my drive for school is back. I like the thought of becoming smarter, that when somebody has a question, their first thought would be to come to me. It is awesome to have knowledge, but in those times when stress does hit, a piece of advice for myself and all of those reading this, is to talk about it. A closed mouth does not get fed. You do not have to handle everything on your own. It is not you who makes you super, it is those around you who give you that ability. It is hidden in their compliments, their words of approval, and their words of understanding, letting you know that you are not on your own. If this is not something you have in your life, go find it. Go find the crowd that will cheer you on and point you in the right direction.

This is what helps me and continues to help me through, not just school, but living every day.

Surround yourself with cheerleaders, but also encourage yourself. If you want others to believe in you, you first must believe in yourself. Life is full of trouble; but this is a battle, and together we will win.

STRUGGLES
BY CHERRY THU

I knew that college was going to be difficult, but I was never sure how hard. I knew that there was going to be a lot of work that I would have to do in class and on my own time. I also knew that I was going to need resources like where to get rental stuff (laptops, calculators, etc.) but didn't know where to find them. Also, who could I go to talk to when I needed guidance and advice?

I struggled with my classes first semester because I didn't know what I was doing half the time and I wasn't studying as much as I should have. One class I really struggled with was my Intro to Japanese class. Learning a new language is hard enough, but having that on top of statistics was an absolute nightmare! Maybe it's because I already speak two languages (English and Burmese), that I underestimated how much work I would be doing in my Japanese class. I was memorizing 10 to 13 new vocabulary terms each night, so I could take a quiz the next day. I was doing 2 pages of translation book work every day, having to make skits in Japanese, and also having to memorize those lines.

One day, the stress got to me so much that I sat down on a bench and started to cry. I honestly thought I was going to fail my course. I was too deep into the semester to drop and that made me feel like a failure to even be thinking about quitting. At one point, a woman walked by and asked if I was OK. I nodded and she left. Then, she came back and gave me the phone number for the free counseling on-campus. I ended up calling my boyfriend, but it was nice to know I had someone else I could talk to, too. I thought to myself, "Your tears are not gonna finish your work." So, I cried my heart out on that bench, got up, and went straight back to working on my Japanese.

I really didn't know what I was getting myself into when I signed up to take Japanese, but I managed to get through all of it, only because I didn't give up. That semester was dreadful and I was extremely happy when it was all over. I'm proud to say that I managed to pass that class with a B-. I may have discussed a lot of how much work I had to do, and that may scare you, but don't be afraid. You can't expect to build yourself up, if you don't challenge yourself in the process. If you assume a class will be easy, stop it. Don't ever assume anything is easy, don't assume anything at all. The best thing you can do is go into your classes with a blank slate and an open mind. You won't get far if you keep thinking this is easy or oh that's too hard. You have to put in the hours to get the work done, and the grades you want. If I'm capable, then you are too.

THE ROAD TO COLLEGE
BY ANDREW BECKER

At a very young age, I knew I was going to college. There was no question about it. The motivation was uncanny. However, obstacles and distractions surrounded me, telling me that I wasn't good enough to go. I tried to ignore them, but it wasn't easy.

I should start where it all began: with a young, sixteen year old girl and a nineteen year old boy who was always chasing the money, any way possible, even if it was illegal. Those were my parents. My dad wasn't even there the day I was born due to the fact that he was incarcerated. I'm not sure if it was the first time he was ever in jail, but I know it wasn't his last. He was out of jail long enough for my mom and dad to have another child, my brother, but soon he got put back in and would be out of my life for the remainder of my childhood. With my dad gone, my mother became supermom, working 50 hours a week to make sure I had the clothes I needed, the school supplies I needed, and food on the table every night. Growing up without a dad was hard, but my mom stepped up, filling the role of both parents. I could never re-pay her for her actions and I'll be forever grateful for her.

Without much of a father figure and my mom working seven days a week, I didn't have the guidance that one would need in order to not get in trouble. For most of my life I lived in poverty, in neighborhoods where there was violence and drugs. At a young age I got consumed in the lifestyle that I was surrounded by. I loved it. I loved having respect, money and power. I hung around gangs because they accepted me when no one else did. I stayed in trouble, not only in school but with the law as well. I got suspended from school every few months and had the police at my mom's door more times than I would like to admit.

I was surrounded by people that didn't even finish high school, working in factories or selling drugs, doing anything to make a quick dollar. When I was young, I was mesmerized by all the things these people that hadn't even finished high school had: all the money they had. It was like school didn't even matter; making money was easier than high school anyway. Everything around me was telling me that education was relative, that you didn't need a diploma to be successful. All you had to do was hustle.

Despite everything going against me, I knew I was going to graduate high school. I had always been smart and every teacher I had told me so. They told me that I had way too much potential to let it go to waste on the streets and I believed them. Graduating high school wasn't a cake walk by any means. Being in football helped a lot, though, motivating me to be a better person. My head coach, Coach Dawson, was the first person I ever saw as a father figure. He taught me how to be a man with integrity, instead of someone with no hope.

The hardest part about high school was during my junior year when I got expelled for possession of illegal drugs. My heart broke knowing I wouldn't be able to play football my senior year. I was so hurt, I promised to never return to that school and continue my high school career at another school, which I did. It was difficult going to a different school my senior year and missing some key credits needed to graduate. But I worked hard and I was able to graduate with academic honors.

During my senior year, I applied to four different schools, but I would always get a return letter saying that there was something wrong with my application. It was frustrating to me and at one point, I was so overwhelmed by applications that I was over it. I gave up on going to college; it wasn't worth it. Then one day a letter from IPFW came in the mail and all I could think was, "What is wrong now?" But instead I got an acceptance letter. I could not be happier. I really did it, I was going to college!

Now that I am in college, I've been presented with another challenge: being a broke college student. Ever since I was sixteen, I have been working, so not having disposable income was something new to me. I had to make changes in order to accommodate being without money for a while. I learned to use Ramen noodles as a filler and to put eggs in everything because they're a great, cheap protein. I also snack less, buy generic cereal instead of Kellogg's and eat out of small bowls instead of large ones. It has been a little difficult, but I managed, and now, with a lot of rationing, I am able to work with what I have.

My road to college hasn't been the easiest by any means. There have been many obstacles and challenges that I had to work through in order to make it as far as I have. I'm happy I am in college and I'm excited for the opportunities that will come because of it. College has been a blessing and if I had to go through it all again, I'd make the same decisions because they got me here today.

LIVING THE "PERFECT COLLEGE EXPERIENCE"
BY MIRANDA HALL

Ever since I was a little girl, I dreamed of the perfect college experience. I would get into a nice school, live in the dorms, become best friends with my roommates, and live the normal picture perfect college life. Graduating in four years was also a part of that dream. But like always, I learned that life does not always go as planned.

What I experienced was far from what I ever imagined. I had 3 roommates, two of which were a year older than me. The other roommate was my age and she was the one I was going to share my bedroom with. Everything went like I planned at first. We all got along and it seemed like it would be a pretty great year. But then my older roommates started to party. Not just a single night here or there either, but more of an almost every night thing. This would consist of lots of people I didn't know in my apartment for long periods of time and they were all very loud and pretty much screaming. I get that partying can be fun, but really it's a Tuesday night. How is that fun? This forced me to leave my own apartment a lot to go study elsewhere because of how loud it was, and for the most part I didn't even like staying there. The roommate who was my age and who was supposed to share a room with me, found a guy and she moved in with him in a few days. This made me feel alone and somewhat unsure of what to do. I didn't want to be that snitch that gets everyone in trouble, because I wanted to be friends. I also didn't want to move because I felt like they wouldn't want to be friends either. So wanting to be friends with them caused me to stay where I was.

All the parties weren't the even worst part, getting bedbugs was. Yes, ewww, I know, but my apartment ended up getting bed bugs because of all the random party people who came over all the time. This caused me to miss many classes because of having to fix the problems that my roommates brought me into with their choices. This in turn effected my overall grades that semester and meant I had to retake two classes. Having to retake those two classes threatened my four year plan and I had to take summer school to stay on track.

Now, I am living with another friend off campus and I am a lot happier. I have gotten my GPA and classes in check where I should still be able to graduate in 4 years. I now have OCD cleaning ways and am very weary about who I live with because of what I went through my first year. But it also has made me a stronger person, knowing that no matter what is thrown at me, I can handle it.

I let my roommates effect my future just because I was worried that they wouldn't like me if I left or said something. I put what they thought of me over what was really important to me, which is graduation. I learned that no matter what may be going on, if they are real friends they will still like you even if you move somewhere else or need some study time. Also, I learned that you cannot plan your entire life out, because once you think you did, everything changes. College may not be perfect but it is still some of the best times of your life. Make the most of it whenever you can, while you can.

DE-PRESS-ON
BY TIFFANY LACKEY

The biggest issue I've had to deal with while attending college has been my depression. It effects every aspect of my life, and has made certain things more difficult than they need to be, most notably making friends and handling college coursework. No two people develop their depression exactly the same; and for me, it was a toxic mixture of extreme bullying, genetics, and the denial of my sexuality.

I've always been the fat, quiet kid, which made me a prime target for bullies. I can remember being bullied as far back as kindergarten and can remember developing—what has since been identified as depression—as early as the third or fourth grade. At the time, I didn't know that feeling the way I felt was part of a bigger issue. I just thought that everyone felt this way; and because of that, I didn't have any appropriate coping mechanisms or ways to deal with the depression. Around the fifth grade is when I first told a family member that my sexuality might not be what they thought it was and that was met with nothing but resistance. I was told I didn't know what I was talking about and that my feelings were invalid, which sent me over the edge. I was about 10 when I began seeing the school therapist and contemplated suicide for the first time.

Fast forward to 18 year old me going off to college for the first time, with what I thought was a good handle on my depression. It was also the first time, in a long time, I wasn't working with someone to keep my depression under control. I roomed with my best friend at the dorms for the first year; and at the beginning, it was pretty great. Neither of us really knew anyone else at the college, so we spent the majority of our free time together. I didn't talk to anyone in my classes the first year because that's what quiet kids do, but my roommate began making friends almost immediately. She was also doing way better than I was academically; and I started to compare myself to her which was not good. I began to retreat more into myself, cutting off my contact with the only friend I had. I stopped going to classes, and subsequently my grades began to suffer which fueled my comparison to my best friend. It just became a terrible, never ending cycle. I came out to more and more people in my family hoping that all of this was some sort of internalized homophobia that I was harboring towards myself; thinking that if I was out, it would all go away. Although the majority of the family members' responses were comforting and reassuring, the only person I was looking for validation from kept telling me I didn't know what those words meant, that I was doing it because my friends were gay and I wanted to be cool like them, that everyone experiments in college and it's a phase I'll grow out of.

My best friend was my saving grace that first year. She dragged me to hang out with her new friends. She always invited me to go out with them and tried her best to get me out of the deep hole I was spiraling down in to. But by the end of the year, our relationship was strained, and I was thinking about dropping out because it felt like I didn't belong. That's when my roommate told me about TRIO. She had been in the program for a little while and really liked it. She had tried a few times to get me in to talk to one of the academic coordinators, but I was never really interested. I must have been having an unusually pleasant day because I finally broke down and contacted them. The first coordinator I talked to was very interested in my academics and she had me running all over campus to talk to a million people about making sure I would still be able to attend the following year. She left shortly after I became involved with TRIO, so my file was given to another coordinator in the office. He was much more interested in how I was doing as a whole, both mentally and academically, than the previous coordinator I was in contact with. It took a while to really open up to him, but once I did, he brought so much information to my attention that I didn't even know was out there. It still took me a year or so to utilize it, but at least I knew it was there.

Things started to head in an upswing after joining TRIO, but it was only a matter of time before my depression started to take hold again. I stopped going to classes again. I stayed in my room more and more and just sort of became reclusive like in the past. After being deep in it for a week or two, I contacted my TRIO advisor and finally asked for help. He had me come in and we sat in his office and went over what my options were. I made an appointment with the counseling center on campus and made plans to talk to my professors which was the scariest part. It's one thing to talk to a professional about your mental illness; it's another to talk to your professors so they don't think you're just blowing off class. It's hard and it's awkward; but I'm so glad I did it because they were all overwhelmingly understanding and supportive and worked with me to make sure I would finish their classes strong.

From the time I had the meeting with my TRIO advisor where he helped me get all my ducks in a row, I started meeting with my professors and talking with them briefly about my depression, just to make them aware. And I have gone to counseling at the college up until I recently graduated. Although I'm in a much better place mentally than I was when I first started college, it's a daily struggle that I'll have to deal with my whole life. Like a chronic pain, it's always there. Most days, it's a manageable dull throb; other days, it's like it's not even there. And still other days, it takes everything I've got to get out of bed because I don't want to exist. But I work every day to make sure those days are few and far between. With the help of the professionals I've seen, the friends I've made in college that are in similar situations, and the fantastic people I work with; I'm kicking depression's ass. I've been an officer of a student organization. I've planned a trip for a group of students who went to Puerto Rico (which I'm told they loved!); and I've got no plans to let depression stop me.

TO GIVE IS TO RECEIVE
BY GABRIELA ROMO

Growing up in a low-income family of six in a trailer park, I didn't see many opportunities. However, my mother would always tell me that when the time did come and a life-changing opportunity was offered, I should take it. Not only take it, but "give them the best you got and show them how grateful you are." For me, that life-changing opportunity was IPFW.

The first two years were rough as I was trying to fit in as a Latina, first-generation college, student-athlete. It was difficult for my family to accept the fact that I was away from home and I couldn't help as much. They made me feel selfish and that I was shirking my responsibilities. In order to suppress those feelings, I buried myself in academics and soccer. I tried to find a family within my soccer team, however they misinterpreted my cultural behaviors. They thought I was too "touchy" for them. I didn't have anyone from my family to whom I could talk about my day because they couldn't understand the college life. When I would call home, they talked about things that they needed help with and my little siblings would accuse me of leaving them and not caring about them anymore. They thought I was having fun and partying because of the way the media portrays college life.

One day in my third semester, it hit me. I was not happy. I didn't have my family. I didn't have a campus family, either. All at once I was dealing with a relative's death, a severe concussion, my father's unfair discharge from work, my brother's surgery, financial problems, the IRS and soccer team drama. I needed a break but I couldn't take one because it was barely September. My TRIO advisor helped me see the light at the end of the tunnel and helped me overcome those obstacles. That was when my mom's advice came back to me. IPFW not only gave me the opportunity to reach my dreams but also helped and supported me and what was I doing to show them how appreciative I was? Despite the challenges I was going through, I decided to get involved and give IPFW the best that I could give.

In addition to playing forward for the soccer team, I joined the IPFW student senate. Currently, I am the vice president of Global Health Initiative, treasurer for Hispanos Unidos and am an Ambassadon. Throughout the year, I volunteer as a Spanish translator at Fort Wayne Community Schools and at the Matthew 25 Clinic. Last summer, I went to Ecuador and volunteered as a surgery assistant at the San Lorenzo Clinic. Once I started giving back to the campus and community, I found it easier to feel like I fit in here. I'm now entering my senior year and am planning to apply to medical school so I can fulfill my dream of helping low-income and minorities have access to better health care.

Nearly half of IPFW's students are first-generation college students. Many of us have daily battles, but those who have a little extra to give, do so through service. My service to this university and community makes me happy. I am proud to be a Don.

A YEAR OF FOUNDATION
BY GILCHRIST "RICHIE" AVIAH

Freshman year of college is the year of foundation. My first year of college was very hard and full of surprises. Originally from Togo in West Africa, I moved to the United States with my mother at the age of 15 to join my father who had been living here the past 5 years. I started my freshman year of high school in Maryland then moved to Indiana finishing my junior and senior year at Pike High School where I graduated from in June 2013.

Moving from Africa to the United States was a big change in my life. I had to adapt to many things such as the cold winter weather, the language and basically start all over again by making new friends. I was born in Togo but raised in Benin. As a child, I was already speaking three languages: Ewe was the native language of my dad spoken at home, Fon was the native language of my mother and French was the language we were taught at school. I also took some English classes before I came to the United States and that was when I realized that I was kind of gifted at picking up languages. When I moved to the U.S, it only took me about seven months to be able to understand and speak English. Many people, especially my parents, were very shocked on how quickly this happened.

One activity that helped me learn English was soccer. I made a lot of friends playing soccer at a park right down the street from the apartment where I lived with my parents. Most of them were Africans like me but who had been in the U.S. many years before. I also made friends from Guatemala, El Salvador and Spain. Since we had soccer in common, we quickly became friends and the more I hung with them playing soccer, it helped me adapt and facilitated my learning of the language. After two years in Maryland, my parents decided to move to Indiana and dragged me along with them where I ended at Pike High School in Indianapolis. Again, soccer helped me fit-in and I terminated high school participating in soccer all years as a varsity player. During high school, we came to Fort Wayne for a team camp which is how I found out about IPFW.

As a student athlete, I decided to pursue my education and sport at Indiana Purdue University of Fort Wayne (IPFW). Unlike high school, in college you manage your own time and arrange your own class schedule as you meet with your counselor. Being the first in my family to attend college and also not being very familiar with the college system in the U.S., my first year of college was very hard and full of surprises. First, after trying out and making the soccer team, I was told that I could not participate in games because the NCAA had not yet declared my amateurism. When I heard that, I was very disappointed. Being a walk-on and working so hard to make the team, only to find out that I might not be able to play, was not very encouraging. I decided to be patient and trust in God that everything would work out. Even though I was not able to participate, I chose to attend practices with the team while working with compliance. It was more than a year before I was able to fully participate in soccer.

Meanwhile, classes were hard and required more time outside of the lecture to study. My first semester did not go too well. I failed one of my classes and ended up with a GPA of 1.9 because I was only enrolled in 12 credits hours. As I started attending TRIO meetings more often and visiting my advisor, I learned how to manage my time effectively. Also, by spending more hours studying at the library and the tutoring center, I was finally able to get my GPA up to a 3.0 by the second semester. Since I speak so many different languages, I switched my major to communications with a French minor.

Now, I am heading into my senior year of college and hope to share my love for soccer someday when I become a coach. Looking back now at my first year of college, I realize that freshman year is the year of foundation. It is very important to do well during your first year of college because classes get harder every year as you move up in your collegiate education. It is also important to know that things might not always go as planned and even if you are not doing well in one or two classes, to persevere and never give up. Always look at the bright side of things and use all the resources available to you in college. I'm glad I did.

FINDING MYSELF
BY TAYLOR HENDERSON

When I was a senior in high school, I thought I knew exactly what I wanted to do. I had decided I wanted to be a neonatal nurse. I had the grand vision of finishing college in four years, working in the best hospital in the biggest city, and making boat loads of money. I quickly found out that this was not the case once I started college.

The beginning of my freshman year went off without a hitch. I was making A's and B's in all my classes. I still had my vision of being a nurse fresh in my mind, just like hundreds of other students. Then, throughout the semester things began to change. I no longer knew if I wanted to be a nurse anymore. Did I really want to work the long hours? What about the hectic schedule? This was hard for me because I am a very impatient individual. I wanted everything to be done right there and then. The thought of not living out this nursing vision that I'd had for so long frightened me. Due to this dilemma, my grades began to drop. I stopped going to class and I became uninterested. I thought to myself, "What is the point of taking these classes if nursing is not what I want to do anymore?" So, my number one tip for college: be patient. I know this may be hard for a lot of people, including myself; however, it is the most crucial part of college.

My number two tip for college: your career does not have to make you a millionaire. For days on end, I struggled to figure out what I was going to do. As I searched through every "Most High-paying Jobs" list trying to find my next career, it dawned on me: why am I searching for the highest paying job? I needed to find something that would make me happy, not buy me a mansion. I finally figured out what I wanted to do, or so I thought. I had decided on medical imaging. I still wanted to be in the medical field, just not nursing. I had always been interested in ultrasounds; however, I was still unhappy. I decided that medicine, as a whole, was not the right field for me.

I was lost once again. I had no idea where my career path was going to take me since I completely left the medical field. Then I thought to myself, what am I good at? I am great at planning, organizing, and getting things done. What career could I make out of this? Well, I was always great at planning parties and events. Then, once and for all, I made my decision. Once I was happy with my career choice, I went to my advisor and changed my major to hospitality and tourism management. After all of this chaos, things began to improve: I was happier going to school. I was doing well again in all of my classes, and I was looking forward to the future.

All in all, be patient and find a job that makes you happy. When I came into college, I was an impatient nursing major with dreams of living in a mansion with a white picket fence and finishing my degree in four years. Then, I thought I was going to graduate in five years with a medical imaging degree. After only a semester of college, I am now a level-headed hospitality major with dreams of just being happy and graduating in five years. The money does not matter. The time does not matter. College is about finding yourself and working towards your dreams and goals. No matter how much time it takes, I know that in the end it will all be worth it.

OVERCOMING TRAGEDY
BY JONNIE WEST

I've always been close to my family. In fact, I chose Indiana University-Purdue University Fort Wayne (IPFW) because it was close to my family, while still being far enough away to let me experience my independence. I've always had a strong support system for anything I've wanted to do. When I wanted to join National Honor Society in high school, I had the support of my whole family behind me, with them telling me the whole way that I could do it. And when I decided to go to college, even though no one else in my family had, I received support from everyone once again. Throughout high school and into college, my grandpa had been suffering from cancer, so when I went away to college, it was hard to leave him behind, not knowing when or if I would see him again.

So when he passed away in November of 2013, just three months into my first year of college, I was heartbroken. I took a week off of school and didn't know how I would continue with my studies. But I pulled myself together and was doing much better, when in January of 2015, not even a month into the spring semester of my second year, my grandma passed away unexpectedly. That was the worst phone call I've ever gotten.

Her death hit me harder than my grandpa's since he had cancer and was gradually declining each time I saw him; she passed away from a heart attack at age of 64. I took another week off of school and tried to keep myself together to be able to return to my classes. I was able to come back and I threw myself into my studies so I wouldn't think of her being gone. I attended classes, completed my homework, and took up hobbies like reading more often and crafting to keep my mind occupied. It was very difficult because after my classes, we used to talk on Facebook and talk on the phone almost every day; it was hard to move on knowing I wouldn't get those messages or calls anymore. I did anything I could think of to not let my mind wander to the fact that I would no longer be able to talk with her.

After all of this occurring, I wondered how I would continue on with everything, especially attending class and completing homework every day. I dug down deep inside of myself and found the strength to keep going. Now, I am almost finished with college and thanks to dual credits earned in high school, I'm finishing in three years. What kept me going was a promise I made to my grandparents; after I graduated high school, I promised them I would finish college no matter what. While I didn't think I'd have to do it without them, I have and it's all because of them.

In Loving Memory of Wendell "Sonny" West (09/24/39-11/08/13) and Sharon West (08/15/50-01/28/15)

NO REGRETS
BY AMBER DAVENPORT

Have you ever wanted something so bad you would do anything to get it? This story is just about that, but it is something that I hope many of you can relate to. I will be taking you through the first couple years of my life in college and how I wanted something so bad, and how I worked hard to get there. I hope everyone in every major can relate to this story and I also hope it gives someone confidence that they can do whatever they want to do.

I had a passion to be a nurse since I was a little girl. It started when my grandmother got breast cancer, and she told me that the only things that got her though this hard time was her family and the friendly medical staff she had. Going through this process with her I got to see how a nurse can really change someone's life. I wanted to be that person who gets someone though what could be the hardest time in their life, but I had no idea what I was getting myself into.

My parents both didn't go to college until I was older and my mother went to an online college. I had no idea how fun, scary, and hard college could be. It was a place where I couldn't depend on my parents to tell me to study or to do my homework and, though this didn't set me back too much, I had to find new ways to study. In doing this I had the best GPA of my life and thought I was ready to apply to the nursing program. I remember waiting and waiting to hear back from the department; and when I opened the email, the beginning line said what no one wants to see: "I regret to inform you that...." I was so devastated I didn't know what I was going to do, but I remembered my goal and talked to my advisors. I was told to retake some classes and try again mid semester, so that's what I did. I got my grades up even more feeling very confident that I was going to get in this time. While waiting to hear back from the program, I had some very hard life changes that happened and all I wanted was to open that email and see that I got in, but sadly that wasn't what happened. Of course I was so upset I didn't know what to do. Do I drop out? Do I try again next time? Do I try a new school? I didn't know. All I knew is this is what I wanted to do and I didn't want to do anything else. This passion was the only thing that pulled me out of my slump to get back at school and retake an intro nursing class. I worked really hard to get good grades in that class and I succeeded.

The moral of this story is no matter how many times you try and fail you have to keep moving forward if it is what you really want to do. This is very true with the nursing program, but it can also be applied with other programs as well. Never give up on your dreams; just fight as hard as you can to get exactly where you want to go. I did and I do not regret anything of the learning experiences and failures I have made because it just gave me more motivation to get where I want to go. I hope you read this story and feel the same way, and I hope this story helps you through the hard times reminding you that everything will be fine in the end if you really want it.

LEARNING FROM THE UNKNOWN
BY ABIGAIL WIEGAND

As someone about to graduate from high school and start the adventure of college, there were lots of things I wish I had known. The fact remained, though, that I did not know what I was doing, and for that matter, I had no idea what I wanted my life to look like. There were no conversations about college, it was always just the next step in my mind of what came after high school. My mom hadn't graduated from college and even if she had, the 42 year age difference between us likely would have made her advice to me irrelevant as it pertained to the current ways of college. Looking back now, I never actually asked my family for advice on how to go about doing anything for college, and it wasn't because I didn't think they had the answers, it just never occurred to me to do so.

Not knowing what career or field I wanted to get into made the decision of where to go to college that much more difficult. I had no knowledge of how to apply for college and honestly I cannot remember, for the life of me, actually doing so. I took my SATs and basically had the scores sent to all of the colleges nearby. I was accepted into all of them; but yet again, I really didn't have anything narrowed down. I finally settled on three schools but had no idea how to choose one. Right as summer began after my senior year, my friend called and asked if I maybe wanted to go to IPFW and be roommates with her—and that is how I decided where to go to college.

Another big decision for me that summer was paying for things. I had received scholarships, but without a real concept of how college worked and how to manage and budget money I was scared I was going to mess up. So I went over to my friend's house and we learned all about loans on the internet. I learned all about types and amounts of loans and signing promissory notes—although looking back I didn't know what any of it meant— just that it was part of the process. I figured it was better to have more money and be covered just in case, so I proceeded to take out all the loans I could.

Freshman orientation came soon after and that was my first time really seeing the campus. Deciding to begin my college career as an undecided major, I had prime choice of classes to take but no idea which I actually should. There was a person in the computer lab with us while we were on the school website registering for classes, and having no idea what I was doing, I gladly and appreciatively allowed him to pick my classes for me. That first semester I met great friends and had a lot of fun, but not all my classes went so well. My math class was the one I had tested into when starting the college process, but it felt way over my head and I didn't feel as though I could really be helped by my professor. I had heard of auditing so I decided to audit the class which meant that I would still learn the material but I wouldn't be graded. I made the mistake though of never going back to the class and this created problems for me later on when it was time to complete my math prerequisites.

By the end of my first year, I had so many new experiences and had learned a lot that would stick with me and help me through the rest of college. I had many struggles as everyone does with learning routines, figuring out professors, and getting used to the workload of each class. As so many people do, I also struggled with depression and anxiety and found myself wanting to drop out by the end of the first year. Many friends I had met dropped out of school and this made me question if I wanted to be there. Around that time I made my first contact with TRIO and soon became one of their students. After I spoke with them for a few weeks and was offered a summer job with them, I was able to make the decision to stay in college. Taking the job and staying in school felt like the first decision I had made for myself and my future, even if I didn't know exactly what I wanted.

It took me about a year and a half to settle on my final major. I switched from Undecided to General Studies first, and then landed on Human Services during my second year. When I was growing up, I received a lot of help from community resources to manage my diabetes and for other things as well. This helped me to realize that helping people was important to me, and a degree in Human Services would allow me to do that and give back. I also found that the material I was learning in my human services classes felt like common sense and college became easier, so I knew I had chosen the right degree for me. It took me five years to complete my degree, minors, and internships but I finally did it and graduated!

Although I made mistakes and now know there were probably better ways to handle my decisions over the years; along the way, I learned the importance of not being afraid to ask questions or make those mistakes. I learned to always just keep moving forward without letting the fear of the unknown stop me. Even today as a graduate with a bachelor's degree working as a case manager at a homeless shelter, I still find myself unsure of what I want. I see it as an opportunity for me to try new things in order to figure it out, and I will always have the satisfaction of knowing that I have a degree and can use it to help me move forward.

OVERCOMING
BY COLBY FLYE

Going to college is a very daunting and fearful task, even more so when you are a first-generation college student. People and family will tell you what degree and field are best for you, when you may not know yourself. You have no guidance on how college should go, nor do you have an example to live by in the family. You will be the one to set a standard. You will be one of the first to graduate. All eyes are on you and your family is wanting to see you succeed and make it. Maybe some want to see you fail, so they can say they were right about you and you were just like everyone else in the family. It's a lot of pressure, isn't it?

Don't give in to the pressure. Face it and conquer it. First-generation college students have just as good a chance as any college student. Don't let status define you and be true to yourself.

I come from a family of people who thrive on negativity. A family where having children early was common or having multiple children with different people was common. I come from a family of drug abusers, criminals, and mentally ill people. Cousins of mine would smoke marijuana all the time, steal, and cheat people--going nowhere in life and making no type of progress. They would often find themselves in jail for cheating, drug dealing, or drug possessions. Some cousins had a child early and had to put their dreams on hold. I have aunts and uncles who are alcoholics that live a sad life with the bottle. One of my aunts is addicted to heroin and left her own children in the care of another aunt of mine. My mother used to have a bad drug addiction to crack/cocaine. This was my family's status and expectation for most of us to follow this path. I did not want to follow this path. I thrived on not going down that road and it was my motivation.

When I was a child, most nights my mother would disappear and not come home for a couple of days and I knew why. Her and my father would fight often due to her disappearing acts; but, I still loved and cared for her. Even now, I love her because she does the same for me despite her past issues. She finally made a change once my father passed away due to a stroke during my high school years. This is another issue I had to overcome: my father's death. Most people take the loss of a parent hard, especially during their teenage years. They may turn to destructive behaviors to cope with the loss by doing drugs, drinking, crime, cutting, or having outbursts. I did not want to go down like that and my father wouldn't want me to, either. I would live for him by becoming a success in life, doing well in school and going to college.

I have been surrounded by hardship, trials, pain, tears, and turmoil; but still, I rise and let it be my motivation. Some people tend to do the opposite and continue the trend because that is the standard of their family; it is the norm. Even if it is the norm, you can overcome it. The pressure was on for me as I was one of the few who had a bright future. I would get high honors in school, I practiced music, and showed no signs of destructive behavior. I didn't want to prove my family's assumption or society's assumption—that a young African-American man would follow the same cycle of poverty and/or crime and ultimately fail in life. I often looked at what I'd been through—what my family had been through—and I wanted to give hope to them. I wanted to give hope so that they could make it. They could overcome the trials, become stronger and succeed. The next step after graduating high school was for me to go to college to prove to my family and society it is possible; but, choosing a major would prove to be another challenge.

When going into college you will have many people telling you what you should go for and what is the hot job right now. Did you know a majority of people change their major several times? My mother was often pushing me to pursue my music and do things with it. I learned to play piano from my father, a professional musician who once played with funk singer-songwriter "Bootsy" Collins from Parliament. My father, like my mother, wanted me to pursue music. But deep down, I looked at myself and realized I didn't have the drive nor the desire to practice my craft. There was no passion. Many people have music as their life; they live and breathe it. So what did I live and breathe for? Computers. It was computers that I found, and deep down, I knew they were my passion. I have always loved computers and technology, and knew how to operate and install things at a young age. I could picture myself actually being intrigued and wanted to learn more about them. It would make me happy.

So you should ask yourself, what do I live for? What is my passion? Interest? What makes me happy? Ask yourself these questions and think through the possible answers. Find that passion and don't pay attention to what people want you to do or maybe what the world wants you to do (like pursuing a certain degree because that field is in high demand). Do want you want to do.

College is definitely a different animal and can be quite scary at times; but if you find yourself and know what you want, you will succeed. Don't give in to your family's status; be true to yourself. You will be the one to set the standard. You will be the one to break the cycle. Prove the negativity wrong and come out stronger and better.

THE THINGS YOU LEARN IN COLLEGE
BY MARTY HERRICK

One of the first things that they tell you when you have depression is "You are not alone." They remind you over and over and over again that there are all sorts of support systems for you: friends and family, therapists and counselors, faith and medication. When you have depression, there are all kinds of people that have been in your shoes, and are on your side.

With college, not so much.

When you're the first in your family to go to college, there aren't many support networks to lean on. No one has been through what you have. In fact sometimes, as in my case, my family is leaning on me.

College is not unheard of in my family. My grandfather was an engineer. My mother is a teacher. But four years of liberal arts education? *That* is different. My grandfather's degree was given after he had already gotten a job as an engineer at a manufacturing company. My mother's two year degree came from an online school. As educated as my family is, there was no one who had done what I had.

On my first day, someone asked me if I knew how hard college would be. I thought that I did. I knew it would be a challenge, but it was one that I thought that I was ready for. I had no idea the things that were in store for me. I had never imagined that the things I'm going through now could happen. I never imagined that I would wake up some days in tears or end others by passing out covered in homework before even getting my shoes off my feet. I thought I had put all of that behind me. I never imagined that it could get *worse*.

I have been part of the Pep Band at IPFW for my entire school career. And sadly, they have seen some of my worst breakdowns. At a volleyball game in 2014, I was stressed, tired and –unsurprisingly- confused. I didn't recognize any of my usual band mates. I barely recognized *anyone*. I stopped a passing trombone player and asked what band he was in. He said 'white.' I panicked. *White!?* I was in *BLUE* band! Had I missed a performance!? The panic got deeper. Our director wasn't there to ask, and he had already said that missing performances with unexcused absences would not be tolerated. If I *had* mixed up the dates, I was about to lose my job. My mind supplied the frustrated words of my mother. *'You just expect me to do for you. You never keep things straight on your own.'*

I started to cry.

The trombone player wandered off, leaving me to tearfully head back to the band building, looking for anyone who might know what was going on. But there was no one. No one at the doors, or the lockers, or the clock-in section. I went from crying to screaming. My mind continued to supply awful ideas. Mom would be furious at having to pick me up again and I would no longer have a job. What kind of worthless, ungrateful bitch was I?

I don't remember how I got into the student lounge. Maybe I thought I could find someone to take me home. Whatever it was I wanted, I was too hysterical to say it properly. I cried and screamed and threw myself against a wall for being so stupid. A few of my friends tried to comfort me. One called campus police.

It didn't take them long to find me, still crying and curled up on the wall. After asking me a few questions, the officer said I needed to be evaluated at Parkview Behavioral. I started crying again. My mind fed my mouth, and I started yelling about my lack of funds. I didn't have insurance. I couldn't afford that! That was way too much money for something that –in my mind- I should have been able to face on my own. It got so bad that the officer said he would have to TAZE me. I decided to wait in the car.

I tried calling my mother, but the best I could do was get her voice mail. My mind supplied all the times that she had threatened to leave me 'high and dry' the next time I needed something. I couldn't breathe. I called my grandmother.

She calmed me down, or at least tried to until my phone battery died. By then, the officer was ready to take me to the hospital. It was a longer drive than I expected, but all I really remember was how annoying I thought the officer was, talking at me when all I wanted was to sit and worry.

We got to the hospital eventually, and I was searched, interviewed, and given a waiting room to sit in. I waited. Somewhere off in the distance I could hear crying and screaming and hospital noises. Every so often a nurse would come in and ask me the same seven or eight questions. I answered no to all of them. I waited.

After a few hours, my mother arrived. My grandmother was en route. Mom brought me my favorite stuffed animal and held my hand. I tried not to tell her about the things my mind had said about her. My grandmother brought me chocolate. The doctors came in then and asked me the same seven or eight questions again. I answered no to all of them. And then they let me go home. I was safe, but shaken.

I had never imagined I would have a breakdown like that again. I never imagined I would be in the hospital over something as simple as stress from school and work. It scared me to know that something that simple could hurt me so much. But it didn't just scare me. It taught me. It taught me that there are resources beyond simple tutoring. It taught me that the support offered by the university for its students was not just there for show. And perhaps most important, it taught me to take the time to use those resources, and keep myself mentally and physically healthy.

I'm in my eighth semester now. I'm so close to graduating and I never would have imagined the kinds of things that I would be able to learn here at college. The sorts of friends I would make. I never imagined being so connected to my professors or my friends. As stressful and difficult as it is, I would never trade this for anything else. College has made my life richer, and I had no idea four years ago by how much.

DAT MAN JOE
BY JOE KRYSZYN

Moving city to city can be both exciting and frustrating depending on how accustomed you are to change. Coming from schools with much lower standards forced me to adjust to college requirements if I wanted to succeed. The No Child Left Behind Act, which passed Congress with overwhelming bipartisan support in 2001 and was signed into law by President George W. Bush on January 8th, 2002, is the name for the most recent update to the Elementary and Secondary Education Act of 1965. A common controversy of this Act is that it did not help reach failing students, assisting them to success, but simply lowered their standards. I agree because I was the student that chose to just pass and not exceed the expectations. I had little goals and motivation to strive for success.

However, what kept me above water was my love for athletics. Towards my senior year of high school, I had track scholarships lined up which was my sustaining motivation. I say "sustaining" because senioritis is a real thing! Though I had track opportunities for the next level, my interest stuck with football and I had dreams of playing for Purdue University. But unfortunate events took place on the field—because football is the number one most dangerous sport in the world—and I tore my anterior cruciate ligament (ACL). This was fine at the time because it was a month recovery and we were only doing summer scrimmages—meaning the season had not begun. But then I completely tore my quadriceps. Yes! The muscle that allows you to get up and down the stairs or squat in general. This was a full year recovery. I was stuck in a full cast from toe to thigh and was not able to accept my pending scholarships.

Though I was upset with life, I came to the realization that this was not God's plan for me. So what was? At the time, I had three options: work my butt off for the rest of my life, join the Marines (which I got denied from because of my knee condition), or continue my schooling. So I prayed and now I am at IPFW sharing my story through the amazing TRIO program. I absolutely do not regret my decision. Since I'd worked with a project manager in construction, I knew what interested me and so I am currently pursuing a degree in Construction Engineering Technology. I enjoy college because it's the hardest I have ever worked for something, it's the smartest I've ever been, and I have met so many people from different places and cultures. I'm proud this is a part of my future. You should be, too.

THE WAY OUT
BY GLADYS CALDERÓN

I wish there was a way to let people know that education can be your way out of almost anything. I grew up in a country in which going to a public school meant running the risk of being forced to be in a gang, or as a female, even worse, being abused by a gang. And it just so happens that one of the most dangerous gangs in the world make a home in my country, El Salvador. The earlier years of my parents were doomed because of the war in El Salvador, and they had a rough beginning, making it hard to get back on their feet when my older sister and I came to this world. Nonetheless, they did everything in their power to assure that my sister and I had much better lives than they did, and they spent a large portion of their income putting us in a private school.

My mother and father knew that there had to be a better life outside of our humble country, and that living in El Salvador may not have been be the best way to raise their two daughters. So, we took an offer my grandma, my dad's mom, gave us. She and my aunts lived in the U.S.A. and told us she would bring us over. My dad was a bit skeptical at first, but he asked us if we wanted to go and of course my sister, mom, and I said yes. I was only 6 years old but everyone who doesn't live in the U.S. has their own idea of it. Mine was that everyone in the U.S. had huge, beautiful houses, everyone was nice and had prestigious careers; the U.S. was a fantasyland.

The U.S. did not live up to expectations. At all. We didn't really bring much, and we had to live with family the first year. We didn't have clothes, and had to go to churches to buy clothes at an extremely cheap price. My grandma called the church "JC Penney's" because each item at this clothing bank cost cents. I was extremely happy each time we went, though, and the clothes were basically free! We lived in about 3-4 houses that year, and they were always crowded with family. We were really poor, I even remember walking around town with my grandma picking up pop cans so that we could turn them in for extra cash.

My first 3 months at school were challenging because I couldn't communicate with anyone, especially about the fears and concerns I had. In my (then) seven year old mind, I came to the U.S. for better opportunities and to go to college. I didn't know how I was going to be successful, but I knew I was going to be. I was dedicated in my education, and I learned English in months. I fell in love with learning. My dad contributed to this because even at that age, he would make homework assignments that consisted of learning the multiplication tables, reading, and writing. There was even a time when he would pay me a certain amount of money per page.

Though my parents had prestigious jobs in El Salvador, they had to start from the bottom here. Their lack in English didn't make it better, and though we had a few resources to help us get accustomed and situated in our new country, we needed certain types of resources that just weren't available. It would have been so helpful to have a financial advisor who spoke Spanish. My parents took any job that was available; they were low paying jobs that required a lot of physical energy, and they were exhausted by the time they got home. For a while, my dad worked 3rd shift, and we hardly ever had family time. All I wanted was to know what it was like to have dinner with my family, talk about what was going on in our lives and about life in general, and have family game nights like my friends. At an extremely young age, I knew we were poor and that there was no money, so I almost never asked for anything. I even worried with my family about money, as an 8-9 year old, those were my worries. Regardless of the stress at home, there was still love, and I was still able to remain focused on my education. College was my goal since I was 6 years old, so there was no way I wasn't going to reach that goal.

I went on to high school and found resources, the most influential being TRIO Upward Bound. My parents and I didn't know much about the college application process, or college in general, and Upward Bound was such a huge help. In college, I also joined TRIO Student Support Services which was very helpful too, mainly because of my academic advisor and all her support.

I'm extremely thankful for my education. Often times, I wonder. . . was it my circumstances that led me to value and pursue education? Was my curiosity and love for learning inborn? Regardless, I am thankful for the drive that I had; given some of my circumstances, I could have turned to other things, I could have given up, but I didn't. I realized that education was my way out. Today, I am more than happy and grateful for my job as an Academic Advisor for TRIO Upward Bound. Education has allowed me to have amazing opportunities, to meet knowledgeable people, to grow in so many ways and I want to help other students who share a similar background realize the wonders of education and reach their goals.

SACK OF POTATOES
BY BUCK JORDAN

From the first time I ever knew there was such a thing, I knew I was going to college. I have to thank my sister, Alice, for that. She was the second mom for my sister, brother, and me. There aren't too many important childhood memories where Alice was not there. She taught us how to jump off the diving board and swim. She took us roller skating. She took us to the movies. She even took us to McDonald's, which our parents <u>never</u> did. Alice left for college in 1985; the second in my family to go. I was nine. When she came back on break, it was like she came back from some magical place. She even drove us 3 hours to let us see it for ourselves. It was a huge campus, way bigger than our neighborhood and there were sidewalks everywhere. I could go on, but IU was awesome. I wanted to go to college too!

Alice graduated in May 1989. That same summer, my two youngest siblings, my cousin and I were told that we would be transferring to a college preparatory school. I didn't want to go, but going to this new school would get me into any college I wanted. Any. College. Period.

Sign me up.

High school was challenging. So many things going on at the same time: classes, sports, girls, social life, home, family, driving. A big challenge for us was that these kids were so different than we were. We came from nothing and these kids had everything. There were so many times when I felt like I didn't belong and that I wasn't accepted for who I was. There were way too many times when my insecurities screamed out: you are too fat, you are not cool, you are not smart enough. In order for me to be happy, I needed to get past those insecurities by focusing on my goal: getting out of high school and going to college. Stay focused on going to college because high school sucks and college was going to be awesome.

....

I can still visualize the view outside my dorm freshman year. Out of the front doors, there was an overpass connecting Storrow Drive to Interstate 90. Below the overpass was a run-down park framed by Beacon Street on the right and Commonwealth Ave on the left. From the rooms above the entrance (like mine) you could see the same iconic CITGO sign seen above the Green Monster at Fenway Park. Charlesgate, as my dorm was called, was situated on the corner of Charlesgate and Beacon Streets. Beacon Street represented the Back Bay area of Boston known for its tree-lined boulevards, brownstones, and upper-middle class living. However, as fate would have it, all my mother could see as she parked on the corner of Beacon and Charlesgate was this seedy, graffiti riddled excuse for a park under the underpass. To her, my sister, and aunt, my college was located in the twin cities of Rapetown and Crackville.

We took out the few belongings I had and put them on the corner. Charlesgate was not open for students yet, so my family could not go up and see my room to check it out and set me up. My Mom briefly talked with my soccer coach and then turned to me with a mustered up, encouraging smile and kissed me goodbye. My sister and my aunt later told me that she drove about 3 three blocks, pulled over, and began crying profusely saying: "I dropped him off on the corner like a sack of potatoes!"

This sack of potatoes still had some tough times ahead of him. Like, when I unpacked, I realized there were some things missing: a pillow, a blanket, sheets, and towels. My dorm had mice, was haunted, and my room never got dark ever (thank you CITGO sign). Orientation was fun, and awesome, and I met a lot of great people. By the end of orientation week though, I got sent to the emergency room. My Resident Advisor said I looked green – which is pretty difficult for a brown person.

So there I was all alone the weekend before classes started. As I laid on my side in the examination room, I remember thinking: this was a tough first week in college. On top of all that, I was on academic probation as a condition of my acceptance to college. I had to work hard at all my classes or else fail and go home, and I hadn't even had my first class!

"You're going to feel a little pressure," the doctor said.

I wondered what would have happened if I looked at life as if I couldn't make things better like I was a victim of circumstance. If so, I should have packed it up by that point. I mean, if feeling sicker than you had ever been while some random doctor is invasively examining you isn't a good enough sign to call anything off, then I don't know what is.

The thing was... I didn't want to go home.

Everything I had sacrificed and worked hard for since high school couldn't be destroyed because I was going to "feel a little pressure." I felt pressure my whole life! Fear my whole life. Uncertainty my whole life, and I made it all the way to the college of <u>my</u> choosing. I was finally free, and I couldn't go back as if I couldn't take the pressure. I finally had my ticket out and I punched it – no refunds! I am tougher than that. <u>We</u> are tougher than that!

We face unforeseen challenges in college. It is difficult. College is supposed to be. My advice to you paraphrases Robert Frost: take the road less traveled by and it will make all the difference. There is no triumph in taking the easy road. Your integrity and your beliefs will be tested. Your faith in yourself, others, God, the Universe and everything will be questioned. Don't brace for it. Embrace it. Learn from it.

I am here to tell you to that you can make it.

Yes. You. Can.

THE END & THE BEGINNING
BY KAREN LENFESTEY

"When did you stop feeling like a child and become an adult?" my psych professor asked. I thought it was an interesting question. My classmates offered answers such as when they learned to drive or when their parents divorced. For me, I felt like college was when everything began to change.

Since I wasn't so worried about my parents' approval, I had the opportunity to discover who I really was. I ate Froot Loops and Cookie Crisp for the first time and blew through my savings ordering late-night pizzas. My dates no longer had to meet my family, I went out with friends on school nights and I could skip class if I felt like it. Some students who experienced this freedom ended up flunking out of college, but I was determined not to let that happen. Fear of failure drove me to read my textbooks before class and to schedule study sessions at least a week before exams.

Even though I managed to keep my grades up, I still made a lot of mistakes. I spent so much time with my boyfriend that my best friend/roommate felt neglected. Unfortunately, we were both so "nice" that we never had a heart-to-heart about how she was feeling until she announced that she wanted to move out. By then it was too late. We both thought we were right and the other one was wrong. We went our separate ways and I realized later that losing her was a tragedy because there's something special about a childhood friend. After all, she had been the first friend I'd made when I'd transferred to a new school. She'd driven me around in her red Pontiac without ever asking for gas money and we'd had sleep-overs where we'd watched horror movies and dreamed about our futures. Eventually I broke up with the boyfriend that had caused our riff, but by then it was really too late.

As with any transition, there were losses and gains. I lost touch with the people who had meant so much to me in high school and because I was quiet, I struggled to make new friends. I went to many different club call-outs and had to put myself out there over and over again. There were months when I couldn't wait to graduate and get out into the "real world." Until finally, I met a group of people who appreciated who I wanted to be. I joined a service organization and made a new circle of friends. I helped sort clothes at the Salvation Army, built a Habitat for Humanity house and donated blood (and then I almost passed out). Doing good things together made it easy to bond. One of these friends is still a big part of my life years later. I started off as her pledge mom and eventually we became roommates. It is because of her that I learned that college offered fun classes such as flower arranging and wine tasting. We have supported each other through grad school and difficult job hunts. I attended her first and second weddings. Since I don't have any sisters, she threw me a baby shower and soon I will be going to her baby shower. Thank goodness I didn't give up trying to find where I fit in on-campus or I would've missed out on so much. I would've missed out on making friends that would last a lifetime.

The main thing I learned during my college experience was that I had to stand up for myself. If I ate Froot Loops for breakfast, it would make me happy in the short-term, but I would be starving before noon. If I cared about something or someone, I needed to fight for it. I definitely should've fought for my childhood friend. If I wanted to meet new people, I had to force myself out of my introverted comfort zone. When it was time to enter the workforce, I needed to show enthusiasm and confidence; I needed to fight to land my first job even harder than I'd fought to earn my good grades. College was about saying good-bye to being taken care of and embracing the fact that I had to take care of myself. I learned that lesson the hard way, but in the end, I learned it. And that's when I stopped being a child and became an adult.

MY MOM, THE VEGETARIAN
BY SHUBITHA KEVER

I'm not sure when—as a child—I was able to discern that my mom was a vegetarian. I'm not even sure at what age I learned what the word vegetarian meant. I imagine I was sitting in second grade and my teacher, a gruff old woman who still wore her hair in an impressive beehive, introduced a lesson on animals.

"Animals can be herbivores, omnivores, or carnivores," she said.

I can visualize my second grade hand raising, "Herbivore?" I asked inquisitively with a tiny furrowed brow.

"They just eat plants like fruits and vegetables...like a vegetarian," she would go on to explain.

And that was when the light went off. My mom doesn't eat meat. She must be a vegetarian. Now I got it.

My mom has always been a gentle soul. She's always preferred to talk to animals and plants as opposed to living-breathing people. I can't say I blame her either. Her limited life experiences when she had me and my sister probably hadn't lent much to trusting many other people. You see, she had us both young. Me right at the end of high school and my sister not even two years later. She was a divorced mother of two before she could legally drink alcohol. I'm sure she spent her 21st birthday changing diapers and working a 12-hour day in a factory. But no matter what types of tough life experiences she had lived through, she was always a positive kind soul who loved plants and animals. I always believed she objected to eating meat because she was such an animal lover.

My mother spent her free time helping my grandfather plant a garden every year. At times, it was modest; and in some adventurous years, it would spread farther than my eyes could see. She would help my grandfather grow a smorgasbord of fruits and vegetables. It was like having our own produce section of a grocery store, ripe in the summer for picking. Cucumbers and tomatoes were my favorite; but together, they would tend a garden that included sweet corn, zucchinis, carrots, sugar-snap peas, radishes, potatoes, peppers, onions, strawberries, kohlrabi, lettuce, green beans, cantaloupe, pumpkins, and—in good years—watermelons. There were even fruit trees and vines: raspberries, black berries, peaches, pears, cherries, apples, and really sour grapes. Every night, when we would have dinner, my mom would painstakingly make sure that my sister and I would have these vegetables and fruits on our plates. "They're good for you," she'd say.

But right next to all the vegetables and fruits, was always a hunk of red meat. Sometimes, it would be a hamburger, sometimes a pot roast, sometimes it would be a ground up version of something I never really understood...a sloppy joe, a meatloaf burger, taco-seasoned meat, a meatball. And on special occasions, we would have steak. Now, when I say special occasion steak, I'm sure you picture some expensive, well-cooked, T-bone or filet minion...but our living-large steak was round or minute steak. And to be completely honest, no matter how hard she tried to dress it up, meat was always my least favorite part of any meal. I just never really liked it. I hated chewing it. I hated how it tasted. I hated thinking about the animal who had to die, so I could be eating it. I hated almost everything about it. I could have gone without it if given the choice; but, I was never given the choice. "Eat it," she always said in her stern voice. And so, I did.

And then one day...around that time that all kids start questioning things, I began to wonder, "Why?" Why would my vegetarian mom make me eat meat? If she was the animal lover I had always assumed, why was it okay for me and my sister to eat meat, but not her? How did she reconcile that within herself? Wasn't that some kind of ethical dilemma? How did she justify that decision?

As a child, I often had many curiosities about people and things, but as a child of a working-class family, I often didn't ask questions. The short amount of time I got to see my mom after she got off of her factory job later than 6pm many nights was spent making meals, eating, finishing homework, and being helpful. Questions were work. And, I never wanted to make her work more than she already did every day in that damn factory. And although throughout the years, I would think about it often; I would never ask. Because asking is work and I just wanted her to rest.

Sundays were adventurous for us. We would drive to the nearest town with a grocery store—almost 20 minutes away from our rural Indiana town to buy groceries. This was an adventure for me because we did few things outside of the little town we lived in. These trips were how my sister and I found out there was something different out there. And, it made us more curious. Before each of those trips, we would cut coupons that my mom would organize in a wooden box someone had given her. That's how we shopped for groceries we didn't grow or can ourselves. My mom made it like a game for me. You match the coupon to the item and see how much you can save. It was a cool game to me when I was young and it made me like math. Pricing, percentages, amount by volume...I was a pro at that before I could drive.

Fast-forward fifteen years or so into my future. Being fed all those fruits, vegetables, and meat must have done something good for me. I graduated from college, and I was the first person in my family to do so. My journey was not without bumps and bruises, but I persisted and I made it through. Graduating from college was important to me, but even more so my mom. She made a big deal out of my graduation and it embarrassed me. I didn't want a big party. I just wanted to get my degree and celebrate at a familiar place. I chose a bar and restaurant I frequented more in college than I would like my mom to know as the place for my celebration meal. I ordered the black bean nachos—because as a young 20-something, I had stopped eating meat too. I told my mom how wonderful the salads and pastas were at this restaurant. She thoughtfully looked over the menu and then very calmly said to the server, "I'll have the steak." And, it was in that instant the epiphany hit me like a brick to the chest. It was like all the fogginess around my mom's vegetarianism just evaporated suddenly, and it all became clear and easy to understand. All those unanswered childhood questions were all finally answered right then and there.

It was in that moment when she ordered the steak that I was transported back in time to a Sunday afternoon fifteen years earlier. A Sunday afternoon with my mom spent cutting coupons and making plans to buy groceries. A Sunday afternoon where my mom would put only things she had coupons for into our cart. A Sunday afternoon where she would look at the price of the meat at the meat counter and choose only the cheapest options. A Sunday afternoon where even the cheapest options were too much for her budget. A Sunday afternoon where she would lay down the family-sized pack of meat and pick up the single-serve portion of meat. A Sunday afternoon where she would divide the meat up between too many mouths. That same Sunday afternoon where she would couple that meat with all the foods she had grown *because we didn't have the money to buy them*. A Sunday afternoon where she would go without so her two children could eat—not because she wanted to, but because she **had** to. She wasn't a vegetarian by choice. She was one out of necessity. She was a vegetarian for me and my sister. And now, seeing one of us make it to the finish line, she could finally have protein for herself. My mom. The vegetarian.

ABOUT THE AUTHORS

This collection of stories was written by TRIO students and staff at Indiana University-Purdue University in Fort Wayne, Indiana (IPFW). Some of the students are freshmen, some are recent graduates or somewhere in-between, but all are part of TRIO Student Support Services—a federally-funded program that offers support to students who are the first in their families to pursue a college degree.

Made in the USA
Monee, IL
05 September 2021

77220750R20056